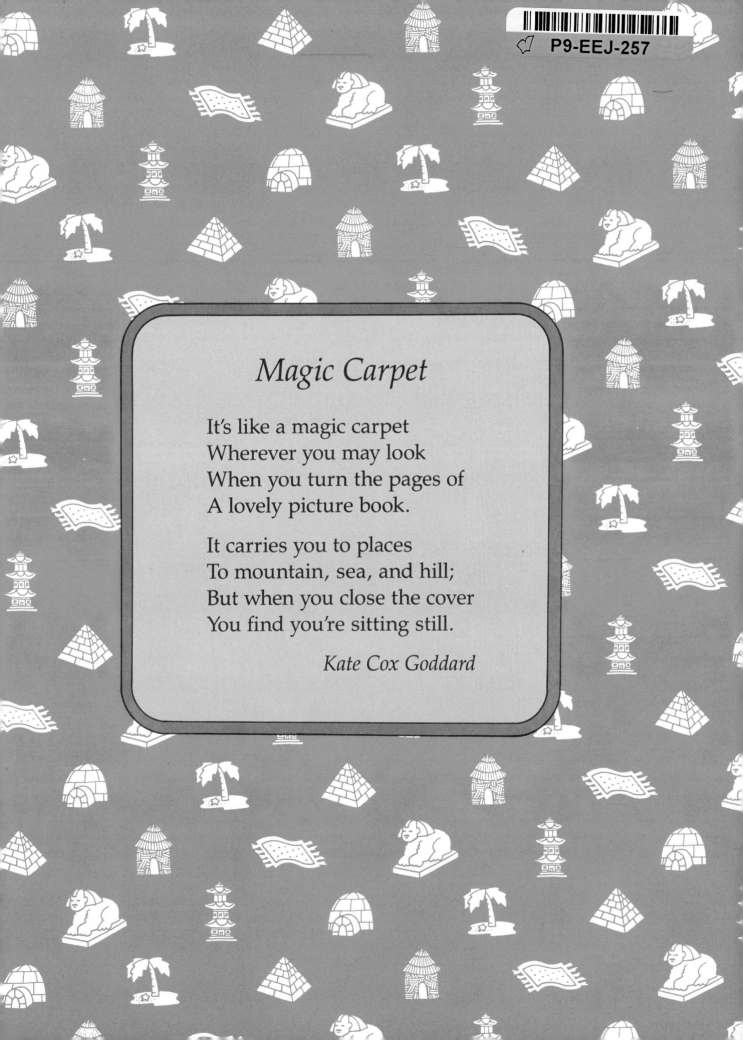

Magic Carpet

It's like a magic carpet
Wherever you may look
When you turn the pages of
A lovely picture book.

It carries you to places
To mountain, sea, and hill;
But when you close the cover
You find you're sitting still.

Kate Cox Goddard

Little People™ Big Book

About
FARAWAY PLACES

ALEXANDRIA, VIRGINIA

Table of Contents

EGYPTIAN DAYS, ARABIAN NIGHTS

TRIBAL TALES, TROPICAL TALES

Families From Faraway Places

Come along, young travelers,
Every boy and girl;
Come along and visit
Four families of the world.

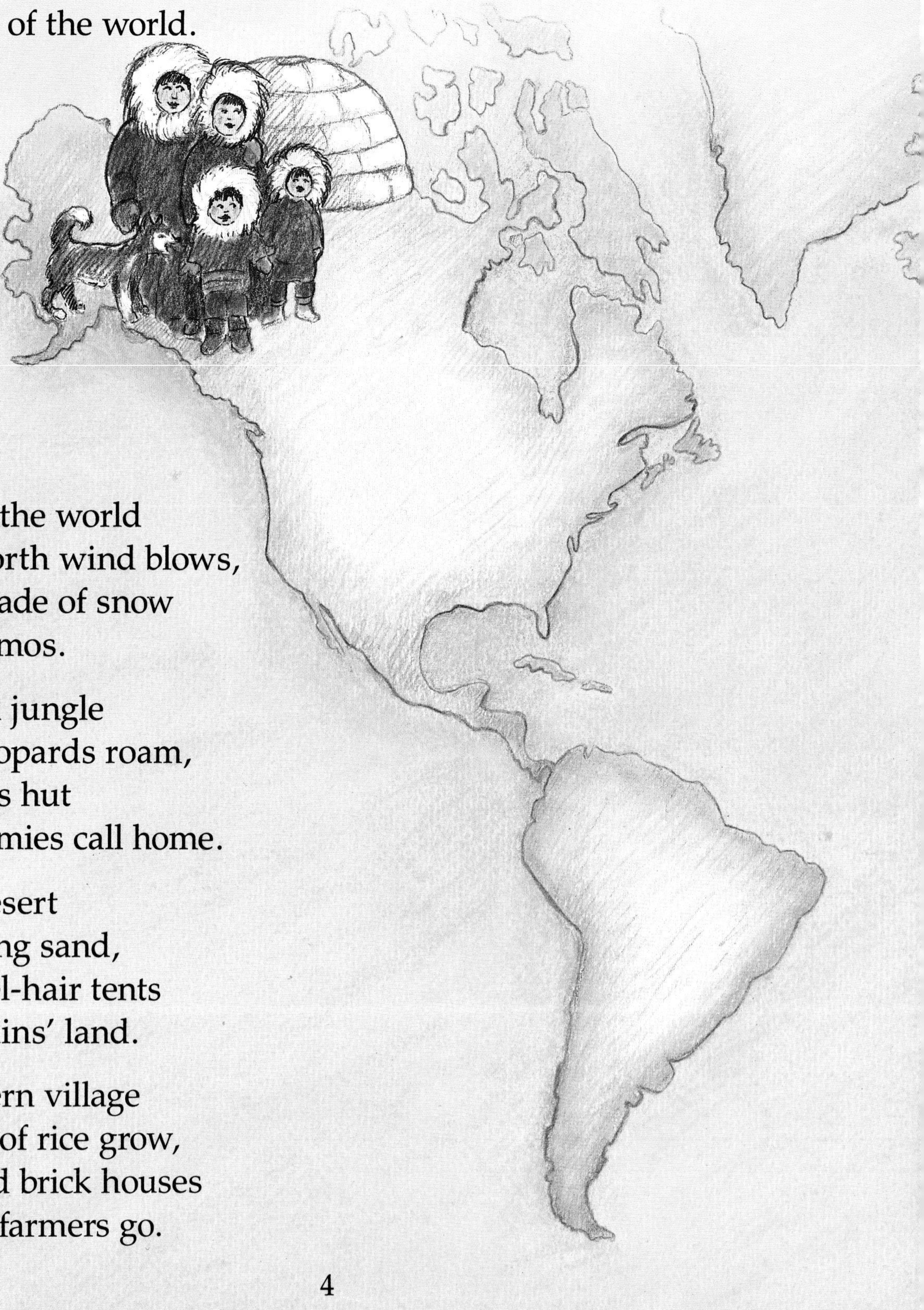

At the top of the world
Where the north wind blows,
In a house made of snow
Live the Eskimos.

In an African jungle
Where the leopards roam,
Is a cool grass hut
That the Pygmies call home.

Out in the desert
On the shifting sand,
Are the camel-hair tents
Of the Bedouins' land.

In a Far Eastern village
Where fields of rice grow,
Home to mud brick houses
The Chinese farmers go.

These faraway families
Seem different, you know,
But people are people
Wherever we go.

Ice, Snow, and Eskimos

An Eskimo Baby

If you were an Eskimo baby
You'd live in a bag all day.
    Right up from your toes
    To the tip of your nose,
All in thick, cozy furs tucked away.

And if you went out for an airing
In mother's warm hood you would go.
    Tied close to her back,
    Like a soft, furry pack,
You could laugh at the cold and the snow.

Lucy Diamond

DID YOU EVER WONDER
HOW ESKIMOS LIVE IN THE COLD?

What kinds of houses do Eskimos live in?
During the winter some Eskimos live in houses made of snow blocks. When summer comes the snow houses melt. Then the Eskimos move into sod houses made from bricks of hard-packed earth. Some Eskimos live in sod houses all year long. Eskimos call both kinds of houses *igloos*.

How do Eskimos keep warm?
Eskimos wear clothes made from animal skins. The animal fur keeps Eskimos warm and dry in the ice and snow. In the coldest weather Eskimos wear two jackets and two pairs of pants.

caribou parka

fur-lined mittens

pants made from polar bear skin

sealskin boots

Do Eskimo children have pets?
Eskimos who live in the old-fashioned way do not have pets. Children sometimes play with the husky dogs, but the huskies are working dogs, not pets. They pull the Eskimos' sleds across the frozen ground.

How do Eskimos catch fish when the water is frozen?
Eskimos go ice fishing. First they cut a hole in the ice. Then they drop their fishing lines into the hole and wait for the fish to bite.

What games do Eskimo children play?
Eskimo children like to play tag and tug-of-war. The boys kick an animal-skin ball to play a game like soccer. The girls use their feet to toss an ice ball back and forth to each other.

9

BUILDING A SNOW IGLOO

An Eskimo can build an igloo in about an hour. Here's how:

1. Use a saw to cut blocks of ice or frozen snow. It takes about 55 blocks to make an igloo that is big enough for four people.

2. Now you have a hole in the ground and a stack of blocks. Lay a circle of blocks around most of the hole.

3. Stack up the blocks in a spiral. The blocks should lean in just a little.

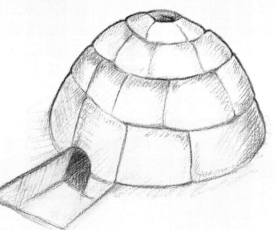

4. Pack snow into the cracks between the blocks. Leave one crack at the top of the igloo to let out the smoke from the fire.

5. The hole in the ground made when you cut out the ice blocks makes a tunnel into the igloo. And it makes a seat inside the igloo.

11

The Sparkling Fire Owl

A Traditional Eskimo Tale

This story happened a long time ago to an Eskimo family who lived all by themselves in the frozen north. The mother, father, and their two children—a young boy and his older sister—lived together in an igloo they had built. The igloo had a hole in the floor for the fire and another hole in the roof to let the smoke go out. Since it is very cold in Eskimo country, keeping the fire going was very important. Someone always had to be at home to watch so the fire didn't go out.

One day the mother and father went hunting for seals, so the children stayed at home to tend the fire. It was warm and cozy in the igloo. The children laughed and played together. But then suddenly they heard footsteps creaking in the hard, frozen snow. Four men appeared in the doorway and stared at the fire.

"We have no fire in our igloo," they said to the children. "We are going to take yours!" With that they grabbed the burning sticks and ran away. When the parents returned from the hunt, they found their igloo cold and dark. "What happened to our fire?" they asked. The children told them about the evil men. "Don't worry," said the father. "We will get the fire back."

So the father took his bow and arrow and set off to find the four men. When he came to their igloo, he found that it was guarded by tall men with long spears. One man with a bow and arrow could not fight all these men. So the father sadly returned home without the fire.

The Eskimo family huddled together in the cold and dark igloo. Then one night the father had an idea. He called for the little owl who makes no noise when he flies.

"Please, little owl," he asked, "will you help us get back our fire?"

"What can I do?" asked the owl. "I would like to help you, but I don't know how I can get your fire."

"You make no noise when you fly," replied the Eskimo father. "You can see in the dark. Fly away to the igloo of those evil men this very night. They will not see you or hear you. You can fly through the hole in the top of the igloo and bring us back our fire."

"I can see in the darkness. And I make no noise when I fly. Yes, I will try to bring back your fire." Carefully and silently the owl flew over the evil men's igloo. His sharp eyes looked in the roof window and saw the fire below and the men asleep on the floor. As quietly as a snowflake falling, he flew into the igloo and grabbed the unburned end of the fire stick in his beak. The owl flew through the roof window and into the night sky.

14

The men awakened and ran outside with their spears. But it was too late. The little owl flew safely out of the range of the spears and straight back to the Eskimo family.

The daughter was watching for the little owl, and soon she saw the fire sparkling through the night sky.

"Look," she called. "See the sparkling fire coming!" The Eskimo family thanked the little owl for returning warmth and light to their home. And to this day when the Eskimo people see the sparkling fire owl flying through the night sky, they are happy. For they know that the warmth of spring will soon be coming.

ESKIMO DO'S AND DON'TS

Eskimo children DON'T worry about having to finish their vegetables!

Eskimos who live in the old-fashioned way hardly ever have vegetables to eat because it is too cold to grow them. Mostly they eat fish and meat.

Eskimos DON'T ask whose turn it is to cook dinner!

They love the taste of raw meat. Sometimes Eskimos eat nothing but raw seal or walrus for dinner.

On summer nights, Eskimos DON'T wait until it's dark to go to bed!

If they did, they'd have to wait for months. At the top of the world, the sun never sets in summer. It shines all night long.

In the winter, Eskimos DO eat lunch while it's dark outside!

The sun doesn't come up at all during the winter months. The sky is dark all day and all night long.

Eskimos DO kiss by rubbing noses!

When a man and a woman meet, they don't kiss each other on the mouth or the cheek. They quickly bump their noses together to say "hello."

Eskimos DO wear sunglasses!

In springtime the glare of the sunlight on the snow is very bright. Eskimos need sunglasses to see well. In the old days, Eskimos wore special goggles with just a thin opening to peek through.

Asian Folk, Ancient Magic

The Firefly

It is a mystery to me,
  How all the summer night,
Without emitting any smoke,
  The firefly can flit so burning bright!

Motoshi

19

Issun Boshi
The Inchling

An Old Tale of Japan retold by Momoko Ishii, translated by Yone Mizuta

Long, long ago, in a certain village, there lived an old man and his wife. They were quite old, and they had never had any children of their own. Because of this, they were sad and lonely. Each day they said, "How wonderful it would be if we only had a child." And each day they prayed to the Sun to grant them a child.

At last a baby was born to them. Although he was strong and healthy, the baby was no bigger than a person's thumb. The old man and his wife were surprised at first. Then they saw it as the will of Heaven, and were content. They brought him up with loving care, calling him Issun Boshi, which means "the Inchling."

As time passed, Inchling grew no bigger. He could dance and sing well, but he was just as small as ever. When he was twelve years old, he was still no higher than his father's anklebone. The old man and his wife were disheartened. And the boy was disheartened, too.

One day, the boy asked his parents for permission to go to the capital. He wished to try his fortune there. His old parents sadly agreed to let him go.

For the journey, Inchling took a lacquered soup bowl to use as a hat, a chopstick for a walking stick, and a needle for a sword, with a bit of straw for its sheath.

His old parents went with him to the edge of the village to see him off. They told him to follow a certain road until he came to a river, then to go up the river to the capital.

Inchling walked and walked, thinking he would never reach the river. Suddenly he met an ant.

"Please, where is the river that leads to the capital?" he asked the ant.

"Follow the path of dandelions, then cross the field of horsetails," replied the ant.

Inchling walked for a long time between the dandelions and across a wide field of horsetails. At last he came to the river.

Setting his soup-bowl hat afloat on the river, and using his chopstick for an oar, he rowed upstream.

When night fell, he tied up his boat in a clump of reeds, curled up, and went to sleep.

Inchling awoke early the next morning and continued his journey upstream. Around noon, he arrived at the capital.

"Finally, I am at the capital!" he thought as he brought his boat to rest at the pier and climbed ashore.

My! What a lot of people there were in the capital! Legs to the right of him, legs to the left of him.

Taking care not to get trampled on, Inchling turned his steps toward a place where there were fewer people, and continued walking.

Soon he came to a beautiful mansion.

"There must be some work for me here," he said to himself.

Standing at the foot of the steps, he cried, "May I speak to someone, please."

An old man soon appeared.

"I am here, under your clog!" Inchling said, seeing the old man look this way and that. "Be careful not to step on me."

The man, who was the lord of the mansion, was most surprised as he leaned over and peeked under the clog.

"But what brings you here, my little fellow?" he asked, picking Inchling up in his hand.

When Inchling told his story and asked for work, the old man laughed and said, "But what can such a tiny fellow do?"

Inchling drew out his tiny sword, and—*fftt*—slew a fly that flew by. Then he jumped up on the old man's fan and performed a charming dance.

When he finished his dance he heard a lot of clapping. It seems the people of the mansion had gathered to watch him dance.

23

Inchling was at once hired by the lord and went to live in the mansion. Most of his time was spent with the princess, the beautiful daughter of the lord. His job was to act as a paperweight, holding down the sheet when she practiced her writing. Another task was to line up the dice when she played backgammon.

Many years passed in this way, and the princess came to love Inchling very much.

One day, Inchling accompanied the beautiful princess and her companions on a visit to the famous Kiyomizu Temple.

On the way back to the mansion, three ogres—one black, one red, and one green—suddenly jumped out from behind a tree. The green ogre and the black ogre clutched large iron rods. The red ogre held a magic mallet in his hand.

Spreading out their arms to block the way, the ogres roared that they had come to kidnap the princess.

Inchling quickly ran forward, placing himself between the princess and the ogres.

"You will do no such thing," he cried.

With that, he leaped at the black ogre and with his tiny sword jabbed at the ogre's eyes until the ogre was forced to flee. Inchling then turned on the green ogre. *Jab! jab! jab!* went his sword. The green ogre soon also turned and fled.

The red ogre then rushed at Inchling with an open mouth, ready to eat him. But Inchling quickly slipped behind the ogre's teeth and with his sword jabbed and stabbed in every direction.

It was not long before the red ogre was crying surrender. Inchling sprang from the ogre's mouth and picked up the magic mallet, which the fleeing ogre had left behind.

Handing the magic mallet to the princess, Inchling said, "Wish on the mallet and your wish will come true."

"Oh, no," she asked. "You have won the mallet in a brave fight! You should be the first to wish on it."

"My greatest wish," said Inchling, "is to be as tall as other men."

The princess then took the mallet and said, "Your wish is my wish, too."

In the next instant there stood before the princess a handsome young man.

Filled with joy, the princess and the handsome young man returned to the mansion.

Inchling's brave deed became known throughout the land. He married the beautiful princess. How proud his old parents were! And how happy they were when their son invited them to come and live with him and his beautiful bride.

A BUSY DAY IN CHINA

The Wong family is out shopping on a busy street in China. Mei-ling is looking at a bird in a birdcage. Her brother, Da-wei, wants to buy a cricket to be his pet. Baby San-san just looks at everything.

Now it's your turn. What can you find?
Can you find three things to eat?
How many bicycles do you see?
How many boats can you count?
Do you see a kite?
What a busy place!

cricket

goldfish

sugar cane

hot chestnuts

rice cakes

Chinese Nursery Rhymes

Little eyes see pretty things;
Little nose smells something good;
Little ears hear someone sing;
Little mouth tastes luscious food.

A wee little boy has opened a store
For serving up food, at his front door.
There's a wee little table, a wee little chair,
Some ebony chopsticks, and a wee bowl to share.

On top of a mountain
A grass blade was growing,
And up it a cricket was busily climbing.
I said to him, "Cricket,
Now where are you going?"
He answered me loudly, "I'm going out dining!"

This little cow eats grass,
This little cow eats hay,
This little cow drinks water,
This little cow runs away,
And this little cow does nothing
But lie down all the day.

Two of Everything

A Retelling of a Traditional Chinese Tale

Once upon a time, long, long ago in a tiny village by the side of the mountains, there lived a rather old and a rather poor Chinese man and his wife. Mr. and Mrs. Hak Tak owned nothing but a small house with a vegetable patch nearby. When it was a good season, Mr. Hak Tak would take a basket of vegetables to the next village to sell. He would then buy oil for the lamp, fresh seeds for the garden, and a piece of cotton cloth to make coats and trousers for himself and his wife.

Now, one day, when Mr. Hak Tak was digging in his garden, he unearthed a big brass pot. "This is strange," he thought. "I have never found anything like this before." Mr. Hak Tak decided to take the pot back to show his wife. But the pot was very big and heavy. When Mr. Hak Tak got his arms around the pot and lifted it, his belt and purse came loose and fell into the pot. "Never mind," he thought. Then he staggered home.

As soon as his wife saw her husband, she said, "My dear husband, whatever do you have there? It's too big for cooking and too small for bathing."

"I found it in the garden," said Mr. Hak Tak. "So far it has been useful to hold my purse."

"We surely don't need a pot this big to hold our tiny fortune," said Mrs. Hak Tak, stooping over the pot to look inside.

As she stooped her hairpin fell into the pot. Since poor Mrs. Hak Tak had only one hairpin, she quickly put her hand in and pulled it out.

"Oh," she cried aloud. "My dear husband, come quickly. Look at this! I put my hand into the pot and I brought out two hairpins, two belts, and two purses, both exactly alike."

The new purse contained exactly the same number of coins as the old.

"There is something quite unusual about the pot," said Mr. Hak Tak. "Let's try a bag of beans."

So Mr. and Mrs. Hak Tak put in a bag of beans and when they

pulled it out they saw *another bag exactly the same size*.

"Let's put in everything we can," said Mrs. Hak Tak. So they tried a blanket, then a padded coat, and lastly a tin of tea. Sure enough, each time they got back two of everything they had put into the pot.

"What a pity," said Mrs. Hak Tak, "we put in everything we could. We now have two of everything, but it still isn't very much."

Then Mr. Hak Tak, a man of great intelligence, had an idea.

"Let's put the purse in again and again." So they did. And after a while the floor was covered with purses filled with coins.

Mr. and Mrs. Hak Tak went to bed happy as happy could be!

The next morning they rose early, and Mr. Hak Tak set off to the village to buy more things with all the coins he now had.

Mrs. Hak Tak tidied up the cottage, and just out of happiness, she gave the huge pot a hug. Just then Mr. Hak Tak returned and startled her. She turned and lost her balance and fell into the pot.

Mr. Hak Tak rushed forward, caught her by her ankles, and pulled her out. But no sooner had he set her on the floor when he saw another Mrs. Hak Tak in the pot.

"How extraordinary," said Mr. Hak Tak as he pulled the second Mrs. Hak Tak from the pot. "How extraordinary!" he said again, looking from one Mrs. Hak Tak to the other. But Mrs. Hak Tak was terribly upset at seeing another one of herself standing there.

"I will not have a second Mrs. Hak Tak in my house," screamed Mrs. Hak Tak.

Mr. Hak Tak comforted his wife. "You're the only Mrs. Hak Tak I want," he said. "But what was I to do? I couldn't leave her in the pot!"

"Throw her back in," shouted Mrs. Hak Tak.

"What!? And draw out two more?" said her husband. "No!" With that Mr. Hak Tak shook his head and stepped back. Yes, indeed, he stepped back and lost his footing and fell right into the pot.

Both Mrs. Hak Taks ran to the pot and each caught an ankle and pulled him out. There of course stood not one but two Mr. Hak Taks!

Then Mrs. Hak Tak, a woman of great intelligence, had an idea. "Listen," she said, "my dear husband. These new people, who are ourselves and yet not ourselves, can set up a house together next door to us."

And that is exactly what they did. The two families lived together in the greatest friendliness. Of course, their neighbors were very much surprised both at the sudden wealth of the Hak Taks and at the new couple who looked just like them. They often said to one another, "It seems as if the Hak Taks are now so rich, that they must have two of everything—even of themselves!"

Egyptian Days,
Arabian Nights

Caravans

Soft, slow caravans swaying through the night,
  Tinkling bells and padded feet, and spices that the
    traders bought,
Easing through the moonlight, over sands dull white.

Hal Borland

THE TREASURE OF THE PYRAMID

Deep in the sandy desert of Egypt, along the banks of the river Nile, sit the oldest stone buildings in the world—the pyramids. The pyramids are nearly 5,000 years old. They were built to be the tombs of the pharaohs, or Egyptian kings. The pharaohs wanted to keep their bodies and possessions safe after they died. So they made the pyramids strong enough to last forever, and filled them with tricky secret passageways and trap doors. Some of the pyramids are guarded by the mysterious Sphinx, a huge stone sculpture with the body of a lion and the head of a human.

How would you like to explore a pyramid? Pretend you are an archeologist. Your mission: Find the Great Treasure of the Pharaohs. It is buried in the King's Tomb, deep inside this pyramid. Use your finger to trace the path to the Great Treasure. But remember, the pyramid is a mysterious maze: Some passages lead to rooms, and others lead nowhere. Still others are traps! Be careful, and good luck!

Sto
Ro

**Beware of the
Eye of the Sphinx!**

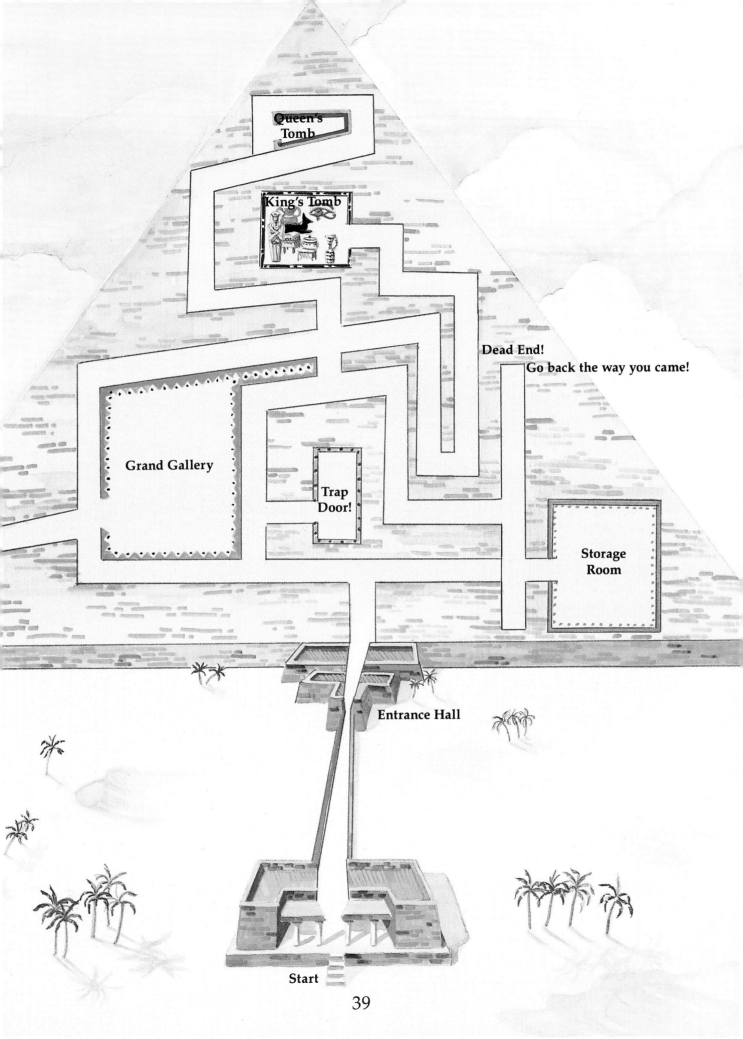

Queen's Tomb

King's Tomb

Dead End!
Go back the way you came!

Grand Gallery

Trap Door!

Storage Room

Entrance Hall

Start

39

HIEROGLYPHICS: PICTURES THAT TELL A STORY

Rainstorm

Wife/ Woman

His Majesty the King

Man/Magician

Water

The Ancient Egyptians lived thousands of years ago. But we know a lot about them—how they lived, what they wore, how they worked and played. That's because they left messages behind them—a record of their life written on scrolls and walls. The earliest of these messages were written in *hieroglyphics*.

Hieroglyphics is a kind of picture writing. Some of the pictures stand for words. Can you guess what this hieroglyph stands for? 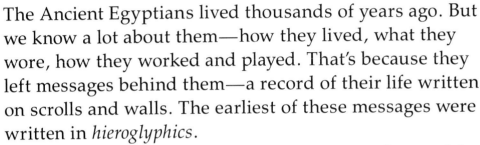 . That's right. It stands for the word "eye." Other hieroglyphics stand for parts of words. For example ◖ is the sign for the "t" sound.

Now it's your turn. Look at the story on the next page. This story is based on a real story from Ancient Egypt that was written in hieroglyphics almost four thousand years ago. It uses some hieroglyphics in place of some words. You can find the meaning of the hieroglyphics in the border around this page.

A Very Old Story

One day [man] was bored. So he called his [servant]. "You should go to the [water] and go for a ride," he suggested. So [man] called his [woman] and they went down to the [water]. It was lovely on the [water]. The cool [wind] blew. The [man] and his [woman] saw a beautiful [bird]. They saw [fish]. Suddenly there was a [pin]. The [woman] shouted. "I have lost my favorite [pin]. It must have fallen into the [water] when I was trying to get out of the [pin]." The [man] called on [servant] for help. He whispered some magic words and folded half of the [water] right over the top of the other side. Then he picked up the [pin]. Everyone was happy. And the [man] rewarded his [servant].

Wind

Bird

Pin

Fish

41

DID YOU EVER WONDER
ABOUT TRAVELING IN THE DESERT?

What do desert travelers wear?
They wear loose, flowing clothing that covers them from head to toe. The sleeves are wide so air can get in to cool them off. They also cover their heads so sand can't get in their eyes, ears, noses, and mouths.

What do people in the desert eat?
Most of their food comes from the camel. They drink camel's milk, make cheese from camel's milk, and eat camel meat. They also eat eggs, rice, bread, butter, plants called *truffles*, coffee, oranges, and dates.

What kind of houses do desert travelers live in?
Since they move around, desert travelers, or nomads, live in tents. Tents are easy to put up and take down. The women weave the tent walls from sheep's wool or goat's hair. The walls are sturdy and keep rain out. The women also weave bright, colorful curtains and rugs.

What do children in the desert do all day?

Desert children help the adults by fetching water, herding goats, and searching for bulbs, roots, and bird's eggs. But, most of all, the children love to play! They chase after rabbits, lizards, and other little animals. And they go for donkey rides.

Why do camels have humps?

Camels store fat in their humps. Since it isn't easy for camels to find food, they eat a lot at one time. Some of the food turns to fat. Fat keeps the hump big and solid. After the camel hasn't eaten for a long time, the hump shrinks because the fat serves to nourish the camel. Then the camel must go find food again.

Aladdin and the Magic Lamp

A Tale from the Arabian Nights

Far away, many years ago, a boy named Aladdin lived with his mother. They were so poor they had nothing to eat. But luck stood waiting for them in their darkest moment, which is just what luck sometimes does.

It seemed like good luck on the day when a stranger stopped Aladdin in the street, crying, "Nephew! My long-lost nephew at last! I am your uncle, hunting for you for so long! Take me home so I may greet my brother, your father!"

It seemed like luck, but it wasn't, or at least not yet. For this man was a wicked magician, who had read in the stars that a boy named Aladdin would help him obtain a magic lamp he had long desired. The magician went home with Aladdin, crying big fake tears at the news that Aladdin's father was dead. But he brought rice and fish and honey for the mother and Aladdin to eat, and they thought their hard times were over.

One day the magician took Aladdin out to a barren hillside beyond the town. "Now, my boy, you can repay me for my kindness to you," said the magician. He twisted a ring on his finger, and suddenly the ground

filled with glowing gems. He stuffed his pockets with diamonds and rubies, and found the lamp on a dusty shelf. Then he climbed back into the bucket and cried, "Pull me up, Uncle!"

But the magician said, "You're too heavy. Put the jewels and the lamp in

trembled. A narrow, dried-out well appeared where none had been before. The magician gave Aladdin the ring for protection against any dangers below, and lowered Aladdin in a bucket, telling him to gather whatever treasures he might desire, but to search especially for an old oil lamp.

Aladdin was a brave lad, and luck was his new friend, or so he thought. So he let himself be dangled into the well, which was really a magic cave,

the bucket first and I'll get them, then I'll let the bucket down for you next."

Aladdin did not trust the magician. He refused to allow the lamp out of his hands. Finally the magician became so angry that he let the bucket drop entirely and shouted, "Then stay there forever!" Then he disappeared, leaving Aladdin alone in the well.

Aladdin was frightened, but then he remembered the ring. When he twisted it on his finger a genie appeared. "Oh, Genie," said Aladdin, "I wish I

were back home!"

"Your wish shall be granted," said the genie in his deep voice. In the next moment, Aladdin was sitting in his humble kitchen, with his mother staring at him in shock.

Aladdin told his mother the whole story. They resolved never to speak to the magician again, for they realized he must have been lying all the time. Now although Aladdin had left all the jewels behind, he still had the old lamp. One day, when his mother rubbed the lamp to clean it, another genie appeared. "Oh, Genie," she cried, "We are desperately in need of food. Can you help us?"

"Your wish is my command," replied the genie. Immediately that day and every day thereafter the genie brought them food. So for a while luck did seem to move in with them, and they were happy.

Now sometimes in stories people fall in love, and that's what happened next. Aladdin fell in love with the sultan's daughter, who had eyes as beautiful as the jewels Aladdin had

left behind in the cave. When Aladdin asked the sultan for permission to marry his daughter, the sultan replied that first Aladdin must build a beautiful palace for his daughter to live in. And he must do it in one evening. With the help of the genie of the magic lamp, Aladdin performed this task, and so he and the sultan's daughter were married and lived very happily.

But not happily ever after, or at least not yet. For one day the wicked magician returned disguised as an old peddler. He wheeled a cart through the streets next to Aladdin's palace, crying, "New lamps exchanged for old dusty ones!" Aladdin's wife thought it would please her husband to have a new lamp, so she gave Aladdin's dusty old lamp to the magician in exchange for a bright new one. The magician laughed with terrible glee and rubbed the lamp. When the genie appeared, the magician ordered that Aladdin's palace and wife be carried far away to another land.

When Aladdin returned home that night, he saw that nothing stood where his palace should be. Gone was his house, his wife, and his magic lamp! He wept and moaned, but luck was with him still, for on his finger he wore the magician's ring. He twisted it and wished, and the genie of the ring appeared. "Take me to wherever my wife is!" cried Aladdin.

Aladdin then found himself in his own palace, behind a curtain. He peered out and saw the magician leering at his wife. But the wife noticed Aladdin and made a sign for him to be still. Then she slipped a sleeping powder into the magician's tea. When he nodded off to sleep, Aladdin and his wife hugged and kissed. Then they searched high and low for the magic lamp. Finally they found it, hidden underneath the

pillows on which the magician was snoring. Aladdin rubbed for the genie of the lamp and ordered him to take the magician so far away that he would never be able to bother them again. And this the genie of the lamp did.

Then in the snap of a finger, the genie of the lamp and the genie of the ring each lifted a side of Aladdin's palace and carried it through the air back to where it belonged. The sultan and Aladdin's mother wept tears of joy to see it flying home, and they thanked the stars for the luck of magic genies. But they also thanked the stars for the luck of having such wonderful children who loved each other so well, for that kind of luck is better than any other. And that's the kind that stayed with Aladdin and his wife for so long as they lived.

49

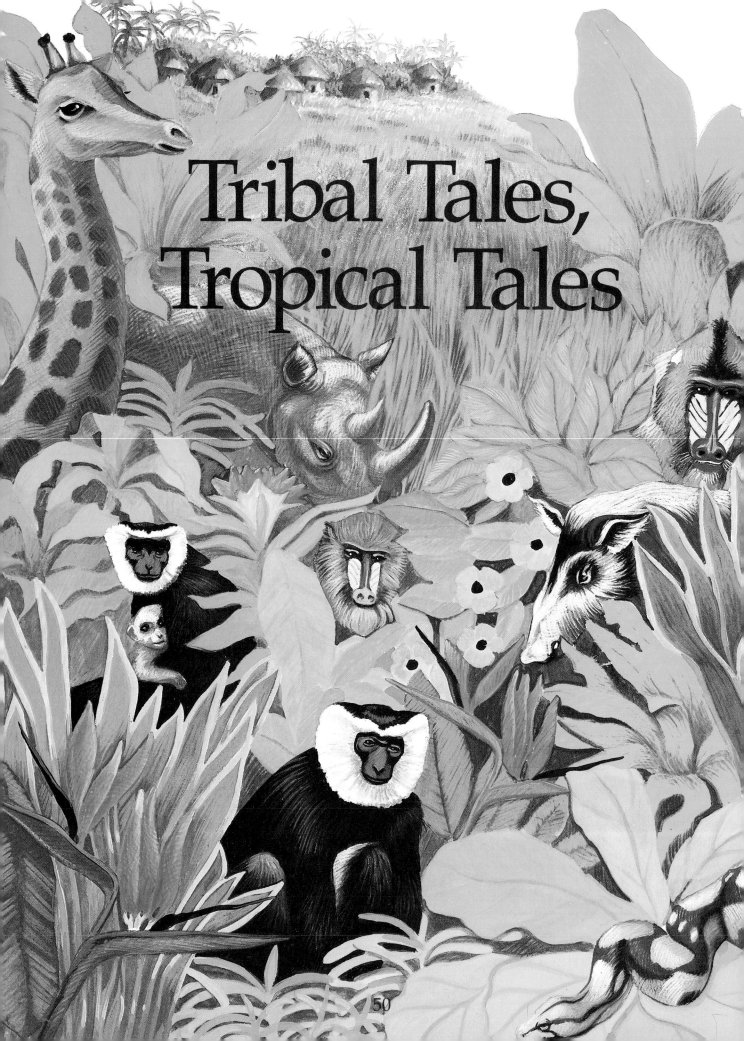

Tribal Tales,
Tropical Tales

Dance of the Animals

I throw myself to the left,
I turn myself to the right, I am the fish
Who glides in the water, who glides,
Who twists himself, who leaps.
Everything lives, everything dances,
everything sings.

The bird flies,
Flies, flies, flies,
Goes, comes back, passes,
Mounts, hovers, and drops down.
I am the bird.
Everything lives, everything dances,
everything sings.

The monkey, from bough to bough,
Runs, leaps, and jumps,
With his wife, with his little one,
His mouth full, his tail in the air:
This is the monkey, this is the monkey.
Everything lives, everything dances,
everything sings.

Pygmy (Africa)

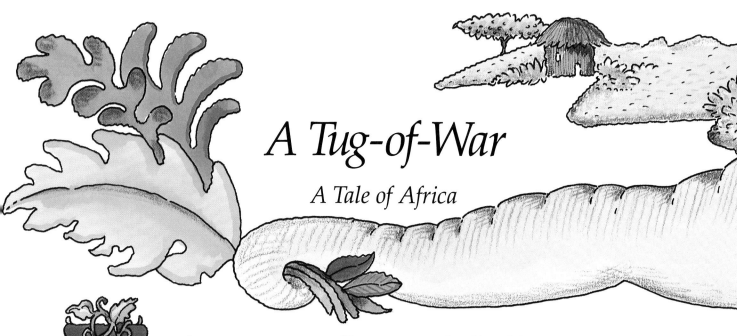

A Tug-of-War

A Tale of Africa

ortoise was a very small creature who lived in a town ruled by the very big. In this town the biggest citizens of all were Elephant and Hippopotamus. They walked proudly through the streets, declaring, "We are the greatest and most powerful creatures in town."

Tortoise was tired of hearing Elephant and Hippopotamus brag all the time. "I am just as great as they are," he said to himself, and off he went to tell them so.

He found Elephant in the forest, eating his supper. Elephant's trunk was a mile long, and each of his feet was as big as a house.

"Hello, Friend!" said Tortoise. "May I join you for supper?"

"Who are you calling Friend?" said Elephant indignantly. "From now on, address your superiors with respect, Little Tortoise!"

"Gladly," said Tortoise. "But you are not my superior. I am just as strong as you are!"

Elephant gave a booming belly laugh and said, "Don't be silly. I could squash you with one toe!"

"I am your equal, and I'll prove it," said Tortoise. "Tomorrow morning we will have a tug-of-war. I will pull on one end of a vine, and you will pull on the other. If you can pull me over, then I will agree that you are the greater. But if neither of us pulls the other over, we will be equals, and call each other Friend."

Elephant agreed to try the tug-of-war. He was quite certain that he would win it easily.

Tortoise handed him the end of a vine and said, "Here is your end. We will both pull until one of us wins, or the vine breaks."

52

Elephant nodded, and Tortoise set off with his end of the vine to the muddy river, where Hippopotamus lived.

"Hello, Friend!" called Tortoise.

Hippopotamus snorted and said, "Go away, pipsqueak."

"I am no pipsqueak," said Tortoise. "I am your equal, and I can prove it."

Hippopotamus laughed and said, "I've got fleas bigger than you are!"

"Maybe so," said Tortoise, "but you can't beat me at a tug-of-war."

"I certainly can," said Hippo. "When do we start?"

"Tomorrow morning," said Tortoise. He gave Hippo his end of the vine. "When you feel a tug on the vine, start pulling. We will pull until one of us wins or the vine breaks. And if you cannot pull me over, we will be equals, and call each other Friend."

"Agreed," said Hippo. So Tortoise left.

The next morning, Tortoise went to the middle of the vine and gave it a tug. Right away Elephant and Hippopotamus grabbed their ends and began to pull. They pulled and pulled all day long,

but neither one could pull the other over. They pulled until rivers
of sweat poured out of their bodies, while Tortoise sat comfortably
in the shade of a tree.

Evening was coming, and Tortoise thought, "Poor fellows. They
have surely had enough by now." So he cut the vine in the middle.
Elephant and Hippopotamus had been pulling so hard they went
sprawling backward. Then Tortoise took one end of the broken vine
and went to see Elephant.

"Hello, Elephant," said Tortoise. "What do you say? Are we
equals now?"

"Yes, Friend," said Elephant, rubbing his back. "Even though
you are small, you are as strong as I am."

Then Tortoise took the other end of the vine to Hippopotamus,
who was rubbing his head. "Hello, Hippopotamus," he said
cheerfully. "Did you hurt your head?"

"Yes, I did," said Hippopotamus. "You are a lot stronger than
you look—Friend."

And from that day on, Elephant and Hippopotamus treated
Tortoise with respect, and called him Friend.

DID YOU EVER WONDER
HOW PYGMIES LIVE IN THE JUNGLE?

What kind of houses do Pygmies live in?

A Pygmy family lives in a round hut made of branches and leaves. They build the hut themselves.

First they build a framework for the hut with thin, bendable branches. They tie the branches together with vines. Then they hang large leaves over the branches. The leaves overlap each other. When it rains, the water rolls right off the hut and the Pygmies stay dry inside.

Where do Pygmies get their food?
Pygmies eat the meat they hunt and the fruits and vegetables that grow in the jungle. They like mushrooms, berries, nuts, and honey. Pygmies use big, thick leaves for plates. Their spoons are made from bamboo shoots.

What do Pygmies wear?
Hardly anything! The jungle is so hot and wet that a Pygmy is most comfortable in just a loincloth. Women sometimes wear simple dresses.

belt of braided vines

belt loop to hold knife or ax

loincloth made of softened tree bark

Do Pygmies have toys?
The children play with carved wooden animals, tops, and whistles made from nutshells or seeds.

Boys play with toy bows and arrows. Girls play a jump rope game with a big hoop made from vines. The girls clap and sing as they jump in and out of the hoop.

Ijomah's Fruit Trees

A Retelling of a Traditional African Tale

nce long ago there lived a family in a village where lots of fruit trees grew. So many different kinds of fruit trees grew there that in every season, wet or dry, there was always plenty of fruit to sell in the marketplace. People came to this wonderful market from all the other villages and towns.

There were four children in this particular family—all of them girls. But one of the girls, Ijomah, was a stepdaughter. Her mother had died when she was twelve, and her father had married a woman named Nnehek. Nnehek had three daughters of her own, and she was very cruel to Ijomah. She made her do all the hard work, and poor Ijomah never had enough food to eat. Ijomah's father was always too busy with his own work to notice. When Ijomah complained, her father told her to be patient.

Now it happened one day that Nnehek went to the market and bought some deliciously sweet fruit called odala. Children in the village liked to eat the red odala fruit, then play marbles with the black seeds. Nnehek gave the fruit only to her own children, and Ijomah got none. But after her three half sisters had eaten the fruit, Ijomah collected the seeds and planted them in her own little garden.

When Ijomah woke up one day, she went to her garden and found little plants had sprouted from the seeds. She was so happy that she took great care to make the plants grow. Early each morning, long before the other children stirred in their beds, Ijomah would go to her garden and water her odala plants. As she watered she would sing this song:

*My odala! Grow
please
My odala! Grow
please
Grow, grow, grow
please*

Before long the plants grew into beautiful fruit trees with luscious red fruit.

As soon as the fruit was ripe, people from all over the village came to buy it. Ijomah wanted to sell the odala fruit and use the money to buy some of the beautiful things that her stepmother would never allow her to have. But her stepmother refused to allow her to sell the fruit.

"The fruit is mine to sell," shouted Nnehek. "I bought the odala in the market and without their seeds you would have no trees."

Ijomah was so unhappy that she could not sleep that night. When morning came, she knew what she would do.

Very, very early the next morning, just as the sun was rising, Ijomah crept to the garden and stood sadly by her fruit trees and started to sing:

> *My odala! Die*
> *please*
> *My odala! Die*
> *please*
> *Wither and die*
> *please*

No sooner had she finished her song when the trees began to droop and wither. Nnehek was furious when she saw the wilted trees. The villagers who had come to buy the delicious fruit were surprised and annoyed.

"My awful stepdaughter did this trick," said Nnehek. "She ruined my trees. She is jealous of them."

Ijomah remained silent while her stepmother spoke, then she said, "But if these are your trees, you can bring them back to life. Surely your own trees will obey you."

Nnehek tried to revive the trees, but they would not obey her. The villagers turned to Ijomah.

"These are your trees," they said. "Will you make them grow again?"

Ijomah smiled and started to sing:

*My odala! Grow
please
My odala! Grow
please
Grow, grow, grow
please*

While she sang, new leaves sprouted on the branches and large ripe fruit reappeared. The villagers were pleased, and they knew the trees were Ijomah's. They bought and bought and bought. They carried away baskets full of fruit, and still there was more to buy. Soon Ijomah was able to buy everything she wanted. Better yet, her wicked stepmother never troubled her again.

Little People™ Big Book About FARAWAY PLACES

TIME-LIFE for CHILDREN™

Publisher: Robert H. Smith
Managing Editor: Neil Kagan
Editorial Directors: Jean Burke Crawford,
                    Patricia Daniels
Editorial Coordinator: Elizabeth Ward
Marketing Director: Ruth P. Stevens
Product Manager: Margaret Mooney
Production Manager: Prudence G. Harris
Administrative Assistant: Rebecca C. Christoffersen
Editorial Consultants: Jacqueline A. Ball, Sara Mark

PRODUCED BY PARACHUTE PRESS, INC.

Editorial Director: Joan Waricha
Editors: Christopher Medina, Jane Stine, Wendy Wax
Writers: Gregory Maguire, Natalie Standiford,
          Carol Thompson, Jean Waricha, Wendy Wax
Designer: Deborah Michel
Illustrators: Yvette Banek (title page, pp. 52-55),
          Shirley Beckes (endpapers, pp. 16-17),
          Chi Chung (pp. 18-19, 28-29), Susan David
          (pp. 50-51, 38-41), Debbie Dieneman
          (pp. 12-15), Barbara Lanza (pp. 20-25,
          36-37), John Speirs (cover, pp. 30-35,
          42-47), John Wallner (pp. 58-63), Randie
          Wasserman (pp. 4-5, 8-9, 48-49, 56-57,
          26-27), James Watley (pp. 6-7).

Time-Life Books Inc. is a wholly owned subsidary
of THE TIME INC. BOOK COMPANY.

TIME-LIFE is a trademark of Time Warner Inc. U.S.A.

FISHER-PRICE, LITTLE PEOPLE and AWNING
DESIGN are trademarks of Fisher-Price, Division of
The Quaker Oats Company, and are used under
license.

Time-Life Books Inc. offers a wide range of fine
publications, including home video products. For
subscription information, call 1-800-621-7026, or
write TIME-LIFE BOOKS, P.O. Box C-32068, Rich-
mond, Virginia 23261-2068.

ACKNOWLEDGMENTS

Every effort has been made to trace the ownership of all copyrighted material and to secure the necessary
permissions to reprint these selections. If any question arises as to the use of any material, the editor and the
publisher, while expressing regret for any inadvertent error, will make the necessary correction in future
printings.

Grateful acknowledgment is made to the following for permission to reprint copyrighted material: The
Putnam & Grosset Group for "Magic Carpet" from POEMS FOR LITTLE EARS by Kate Cox Goddard. Copy-
right © 1944 by Kate Cox Goddard, renewed 1971 by Platt & Munk Co., Inc. Walker & Co. for ISSUN BOSHI
THE INCHLING, An Old Tale of Japan, retold by Momoko Ishii, translated by Yone Mizuta. Copyright © 1967
Fukuinkan Shotan.

Library of Congress Cataloging-in-Publication Data

Little people big book about faraway places.
    p. cm.—(Little people big books)
  Summary: An illustrated collection of folktales, poems, rhymes, informational articles, and related activities
relating to different peoples and places in the world.
    ISBN 0-8094-7504-9.—ISBN 0-8094-7505-7 (lib. bdg.)
    1. Children's literature. [1. Literature—Collections.] I. Time-Life for Children (Firm)
II. Title: About faraway places. III. Series.
PZ5.L72574 1990
808.8'99282—dc20

90-32709
CIP
AC

TIME-LIFE BOOKS
ALEXANDRIA, VIRGINIA

Magic Carpet

It's like a magic carpet
Wherever you may look
When you turn the pages of
A lovely picture book.

It carries you to places
To mountain, sea, and hill;
But when you close the cover
You find you're sitting still.

Kate Cox Goddard